Desserts

Tapioca Payasam

[Serves 4]

This irresistible, creamy tapioca dessert is flavored with saffron and cardamom.

¼ **cup raw cashew halves**

1 **tablespoon unsalted butter** divided

½ **cup tapioca (not quick-cooking)**

3 **cups 2-percent or whole milk**

¼ **teaspoon ground cardamom**

4 **to 6 saffron threads**

2 **very small pieces cystalline camphor**
  optional

½ **cup sugar** more, if desired

¼ **cup raisins** optional

1 Fry cashew halves in ½ tablespoon butter in a small skillet or butter warmer over medium heat until evenly cooked. Remove cashews from skillet and set aside.

2 Melt the remaining ½ tablespoon butter in a deep saucepan. Add tapioca and cook for a few minutes, stirring constantly.

3 Slowly add milk in 1 cup increments, stirring all the while over medium to low heat, until tapioca cooks, about 15 minutes. When tapioca is cooked it will increase in size and will become softer.

4 Add cardamom, saffron threads, crystalline camphor, if using, and sugar. Stir well over low heat. Add cashew halves and raisins, if desired.

5 You may serve payasam at room temperature or as a cold dessert.

If room temperature is preferred: remove payasam from heat, cover and leave at room temperature until time of serving. Add additional warm milk and sugar as desired before serving.

If you prefer to serve payasam cold: put in the refrigerator, where it will thicken. Before serving, place it in a microwave oven and warm for a minute or two. Stir well and add additional cold milk until payasam reaches your desired consistency. You may also add additional sugar as desired.

Carrot Halva

[Serves 8]

Carrots cooked in milk with sugar, cardamom, and saffron make a tempting treat!

10 raw cashew halves or **10 raw pistachio halves**

1 tablespoon melted unsalted butter

1 cup whole milk

2 cups grated carrots

½ cup sugar

½ teaspoon cardamom powder

4 to 6 saffron threads

1 In a small skillet, fry cashew or pistachio halves in butter until toasted. Set aside.

2 In a heavy-bottomed saucepan, bring milk just to a boil over medium heat. When the milk comes to a boil, reduce heat to medium-low. Add grated carrots and sugar. Cook carrots over medium-low heat until tender, stirring often.

3 Add cardamom powder, saffron, and roasted cashews or pistachios. Mix well and stir until the mixture thickens.Pour mixture into a glass plate or bowl and let cool at room temperature before serving.

Mango Lassi

[Serves 4]

Serve this lassi chilled as a refreshing hot weather drink.

1 can (about 30 ounce) mango pulp

30 ounces low-fat cultured buttermilk or
   unsweetened vanilla almond milk

Sugar or **honey** as desired

2 tablespoons rose essence* optional

Rum to taste optional

*Rose essence is used throughout India and the
Middle East for sweets. You should be able to find
it at Indian or Middle Eastern grocers.

1 Put all the ingredients except rum in a large
punch bowl. Whisk until well blended. Adjust level of
sweetness. Refrigerate and serve cold.

2 To serve, pour over crushed ice in a tall glass. If
using rum add 2 tablespoons rum to each glass.

Sweet Black Rice with Cardamom and Coconut

[Serves 4]

A delectable dessert made with whole-grain black rice that's slightly sweet and sticky with a hint of spice.

1 cup black rice

1 cup sugar

½ teaspoon ground cardamom

2 tablespoons melted unsalted butter (ghee)

½ **cup grated fresh coconut** or **sweetened shredded coconut**

1 Bring 3 cups of water to a boil and then add rice. Cook rice about 25 minutes or until soft. (A rice cooker or pressure cooker can be used to cook rice quickly.)

2 Put cooked rice in a bowl and add sugar, cardamom, melted butter, and coconut. Mix well.

3 Serve at room temperature or cold, and garnish with fruit as desired.

Suggested Menus

NON-VEGETARIAN

 Spice-Rubbed Roasted Chicken
Cauliflower Rice with Cashews
Green Beans Poriyal
Seasoned Tomato Yogurt Salad

 Lamb Kulambu
Seasoned Cabbage Rice Pilaf
Roasted Brussels Sprouts
Minty Cucumber Yogurt Salad

Chicken Biriyani Rice
Egg Curry or Hard-boiled Egg seasoned
    with black pepper and ground cumin
Seasoned Vegetable Yogurt Salad

Spicy Seared Shrimp
Black Pepper and Cumin Rice with Cashews
Seasoned Tri-colored Bell Peppers

Fish in Ginger Garlic Sauce
Carrot Rice with Cashews
Asparagus with Ginger and Coconut

VEGETARIAN

 Black Bean Cutlets (Veggie Burger)
Peanut and Coconut Chutney
Vegetable Quinoa
Bell Pepper and Tomato Pachadi

 Spinach Rice with Cashews
Carrot Sambhar
Roasted Potatoes Medley

 Adais (Lentil Pancakes)
Potato Onion Kose
Eggplant Chutney

 Plain Basmati Rice
Bell Pepper and Radish Sambhar
Broccoli with Coconut Poriyal

 Fragrant Lemon Rice
Eggplant Curry with Green Peas
Heavenly Lima Bean Masala

Black Pepper and Cumin Rice with Cashews
Potatoes and Tomatoes in Lentil Sauce
Green Beans with Carrots

FUSION MENUS

The recipes in this cookbook will "fuse" beautifully with Western favorites. Use your imagination and have fun blending the dishes.

❋ With Grilled, Roasted, or Baked Chicken

Any one flavored rice or quinoa dish, such as:
> Spinach Rice with Cashews
> Tomato Rice with Green Onions
> Vegetable Quinoa
> *(or other flavored rice dishes)*

One or more vegetable dishes:
> Butternut Squash Masala
> Cabbage with Ginger Poriyal
> Sweet Potato Poriyal
> *(or other vegetable dishes)*

❋ With Grilled Fish or Shrimp

Any one flavored rice dish, such as:
> Black Pepper and Cumin Rice with Cashews
> Fragrant Lemon Rice
> *(or other flavored rice dishes)*

One or more vegetable dishes:
> Brussels Sprouts with Chickpea Poriyal
> Eggplant Curry with Green Peas
> Sweet Potato Poriyal
> *(or other vegetable dishes)*

❋ Thanksgiving & Holiday Side Dishes

The following vibrant, colorful appetizers and side dishes will bring a unique blend of fusion flavors to your holiday meals. East can meet West right at your dinner table!

Appetizers (Select one or two items):
> Spinach Yogurt Dip
> Eggplant Chutney
> Peanut and Coconut Chutney
> *(served as a dip with fresh vegetables)*
> Seasoned Apple Relish *(served on toasted bread)*

Flavored Rice or Quinoa Dishes (Select one item):
> Black Pepper and Cumin Rice with Cashews
> Carrot Rice with Cashews
> Cauliflower Rice with Cashews
> Fragrant Lemon Rice
> Tomato Rice with Green Onions
> Vegetable Rice Pilaf
> Vegetable Quinoa

Vegetable Side Dishes (Select one or more items):
> Roasted Brussels Sprouts
> Green Beans with Carrots
> Green Beans Poriyal
> Roasted Potato Medley
> Potato Masala
> Sweet Potato Poriyal
> Roasted Vegetables
> Butternut Squash Masala
> Brussels Sprouts Kulambu

Although the above ideas of food combinations are unusual from a purely South Indian culinary perspective, you may find them truly enjoyable. And now you can use your own creativity!

FUSION THANKSGIVING DINNER MENU
A UNIQUE BLEND OF EAST AND WEST

Spice Rubbed Roasted Turkey with Pan Gravy (page 268)
Curried Stuffing (page 268)
Bell Pepper and Tomato Rice with Cashews (page 81)
Sweet Potato Poriyal (page 215)
Green Beans Poriyal (page 185)
Roasted Brussels Sprouts (page 149)
Cranberry Fruit Salad (recipe below)
Dinner rolls with butter
Mango Lassi with Honey (page 263)
Pumpkin or Pecan Pie with ice cream
Indian Chai Tea with Cardamom

Cranberry Fruit Salad

[Serves 8 to 10]

2 (12-ounce) bags fresh cranberries

2 cups sugar

2 (10-ounce) cans crushed pineapple in juice
   drained

2 cups chopped walnuts

2 cups miniature marshmallows

1 pint whipping cream

1 Rinse and drain cranberries. Coarsely chop cranberries in a blender.

2 Mix chopped cranberries and sugar in a bowl. Add the crushed pineapple, walnuts, and marshmallows and stir well.

3 In a separate bowl, whip cream to a firm consistency.* Carefully fold whipped cream into cranberry mixture. Refrigerate cranberry salad in bowl until serving.

*It is helpful to cool the bowl and blades of the electric beater for at least 30 minutes before whipping cream. This will quicken the whipping-process.

Spice-Rubbed Roasted Turkey with Curried Stuffing

[Serves 8 to 10]

10 to 12 pound Butterball turkey (fresh or frozen)

Spice Rub
2 teaspoons garam masala

¾ teaspoon cayenne pepper powder

1 teaspoon ground turmeric

3 teaspoons garlic powder

1 teaspoon salt

½ cup canola oil

Curried Stuffing
8 tablespoons (1 stick) unsalted butter

3 cups stuffing croutons (preferably onion sage flavor)

1½ cups chopped celery

2 cups chopped walnuts

1½ cups chopped onions

6 to 8 garlic cloves minced

2 teaspoons American curry powder

¾ teaspoon ground turmeric

1 teaspoon salt

1 teaspoon ground black pepper

1 If turkey is frozen, follow directions for thawing (instructions are often on the outer wrapping of the turkey). After turkey is thawed, remove all the packaging from inside the cavity of turkey. Rinse turkey thoroughly and pat dry inside and out with paper towels. Place turkey in roasting pan. (Note: You may wish to purchase a disposable aluminum-foil roasting pan in grocery store.) Preheat oven according to wrapper instructions.

2 In a small bowl, mix together all spice rub ingredients. Rub the spiced-oil mixture all over the turkey, inside and out.

3 For curried stuffing, melt butter in a large saucepan. Add all of the stuffing ingredients to the melted butter over medium-low heat. Toss stuffing ingredients for a few minutes to blend evenly and coat with butter. Allow stuffing to cool.

4 Fill cavity of turkey with stuffing, being careful not to pack too tightly. (Note: It is advisable to stuff turkey just before roasting.) Truss (Tie up) stuffed turkey with string. Follow wrapper instructions for roasting.

AMERICAN-STYLE PAN GRAVY (OPTIONAL STEP)
5 After removing turkey from oven, remove it from the roasting pan and set aside, covered with aluminum foil to keep warm. Pour off excess fat from roasting pan, leaving only about ½ cup of drippings in roasting pan. Heat the drippings for a few minutes over medium-low heat, while loosening turkey bits from bottom of roasting pan with a spoon. Add 2 cups of water to roasting pan. Season moderately with salt and pepper. Place 1 tablespoon of cornstarch or flour in a small cup and blend thoroughly with 2 tablespoons of water to make a paste. Add ½ cup more water to paste and stir into drippings in the roasting pan. This will thicken the gravy. Continue stirring gravy about 7 minutes, until desired thickness. Taste and adjust seasonings.

Index

var. = variation

ACKNOWLEDGMENTS

I thank my husband Dr. K. Vairavan (or KV as we fondly call him) for his constant love, encouragement, and support in every step of my culinary journey, and especially during the recording of my television series that bears the same name as this book.

I also thank Sharon Jewell who was of great assistance to me during the production of the television series. I wish to express special thanks to Priti Gress, Editorial Director at Hippocrene Books, for her invitation and encouragement to write this book. I could not have wished for a more helpful, efficient, and friendly editor to work with. My thanks are also due to Dr. Patricia Marquardt, the co-author of two of my previous books for her encouragement and useful comments about this book. I also benefited very much from technical support during the final editorial process from Santhosh Yegnaraman. And I add a note of thanks and appreciation to Barbara Keane-Pigeon for her invaluable assistance during the final editorial and production stages.

I owe special gratitude to my friend and photographer, Linda Smallpage, for the beautiful photographs of the recipes in this cookbook.

Finally, I would be remiss not to acknowledge Milwaukee Public Television (MPTV) for producing and airing my television series that forms the basis for this book. Also my thanks go to PBS CREATE for airing my shows on national television. The national broadcast helped spread the simple message that healthful Indian cooking is within everyone's reach.

Most importantly I want to thank the television viewers from around the country for their interest and inspiring comments that led me to write this cookbook.

ABOUT THE AUTHOR

Alamelu Vairavan is the host of "Healthful Indian Flavors with Alamelu" produced by Milwaukee Public Television and aired nationally on PBS CREATE. She is a culinary educator and consultant with a passion to promote healthful cooking to the public. Internationally recognized as an expert on South Indian cooking, Alamelu has trained chefs and offered wellness programs at many corporations. She has authored several books including *Healthy South Indian Cooking, Expanded Edition* and *Indian Inspired Gluten-Free Cooking*, both published by Hippocrene Books.

Alamelu holds a degree in Health Information Management from the University of Wisconsin-Milwaukee. She maintains a residence in Wisconsin and Arizona.

Visit Alamelu at www.curryonwheels.com.

Also by Alamelu Vairavan . . .

HEALTHY SOUTH INDIAN COOKING
Expanded Edition
Alamelu Vairavan and Dr. Patricia Marquardt

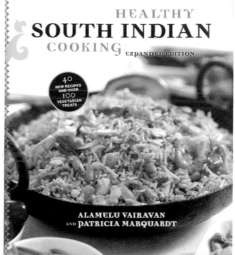

"Coconut-infused curries, brilliant vegetable dishes . . . what could be complex becomes relatively simple in Vairavan's approach . . ."
—Los Angeles Times

"Besides 100 feast-worthy vegetarian recipes, [the authors] explain how the spices that make Indian cuisine so fragrant and flavorful also pack a whallop of nutrients and disease-fighting phytochemicals."
—Wisconsin State Journal

"Dals, chutneys and curries take their place along with fare that might be totally new to many . . . the authors do a remarkably good job of keeping the recipes relatively simple and accessible."
—The Post-Crescent

In the famous Chettinad cooking tradition of southern India, these mostly vegetarian recipes allow home cooks to create dishes such as Potato-filled Dosas with Coconut Chutney; Pearl Onion and Tomato Sambhar; Chickpea and Bell Pepper Poriyal; and Eggplant Masala Curry. *Rasams*, breads, legumes and *payasams* are all featured here, as is the exceptional Chettinad Chicken Kolambu, South India's version of the popular *vindaloo*. Each of these low-fat, low-calorie recipes come with a complete nutritional analysis. Also included are sample menus and innovative suggestions for integrating South Indian dishes into traditional Western meals. A section on the varieties and methods of preparation for *dals* (a lentil dish that is a staple of this cuisine), a multilingual glossary of spices and ingredients, and 16 pages of color photographs make this book a clear and concise introduction to the healthy, delicious cooking of South India.

ISBN: 0-7818-1189-9 · $35.00hc